Chef Lenny
Cooking for Humans

Chef Lenny

Cooking for Humans

The ideal companion for the modern lizard

34 Approved Recipes for

HUMAN CONSUMPTION

Leonard Patrick

Chef Lenny Cooking for Humans

"This is a collection of our family's favorite dishes. I truly hope that you can taste the love that has gone into each one of these trusted recipes. Let us cook!" -Chef Lenny

I am a Pacific Northwest chef, author, and bearded dragon lizard. When I am not cooking tasty food for my human family, I prefer to be in my window bed watching the squirrels playing outside. My other hobbies include scampering, spa days, car rides, and being wrapped in a blanket like a burrito.

What is Inside?

- Breakfast at Lenny's
- Playing with Dough
- It is Soup Day!
- Fancy Finger Foods
- Impressive Entrees
- Dreamy Desserts
- Blend, Mash & Mix
- Social & Inquires

Breakfast at Lenny's

Biscuits & Chicken Gravy

For Gravy

1 lb. ground chicken breakfast sausage

3 Tbsp. butter

3 c. milk

1/3 c. all-purpose flour

1/8 tsp. nutmeg

Salt & pepper to taste

For Biscuits

2 ½ c. all-purpose flour

2 Tbsp. baking powder

1 tsp. salt

½ c. unsalted butter (very cold!)

1 c. + 2 Tbsp. cold buttermilk (1 c. milk + 1 Tbsp of apple cider vinegar makes a buttermilk replacement in a pinch)

2 tsp. honey

Biscuit Instructions

Preheat oven to 425°F. Place all the dry ingredients (flour, baking powder, & salt) into a bowl or a food processor. Mix or pulse in the processor until the blend resembles corn meal. Transfer to a bowl if you used a processor. Make a well in the center of the mix. Pour in 1 cup of buttermilk (reserving the 2 Tbsp for later) and the honey. Stir it all together until it is *just* together. You do not want to overwork it, as it will become too tough to rise properly. Turn out your dough onto a lightly floured work surface. Shape the dough into a rectangle. Fold one side into the center and then the other side. Turn the dough so that it is long ways, or "hotdog" style. Gently press down dough to flatten. Repeat the folding method again, then turn and fold one more time. This creates your layers. When you have finished, carefully roll out your dough with a rolling pin, pint glass, beer bottle or baton. Then with a biscuit cutter or wide-mouth mason jar ring, cut out approximately 10 biscuits and **place with their edges touching** in a cast iron skillet, or on a baking sheet with parchment paper. Brush tops with remaining buttermilk and bake till golden brown for 15 or so minutes. Enjoy warm!

Gravy Instructions

In a high-sided pan, brown the ground chicken on medium to medium-high heat with the 3-Tbsp of butter. Once the meat has cooked thoroughly, add the flour and stir to evenly coat all the meat pieces. Slowly add the milk, stirring constantly. Continue to stir and add salt, pepper, and the nutmeg. Lower the heat to a light simmer and continue stirring until the gravy has reached your desired thickness. Keep in that it will thicken more as it cools. If it ends up too thick, add a bit more milk, 1 Tbsp at a time.

When the biscuits are done and the gravy has thickened, you are ready to enjoy this feast! Pour the gravy on top of the biscuits and add a little parsley from the garden for a pop color. This dish pairs well with a couple fried eggs and/or a fruit salad. **Serves 4**

Dutch Baby

4 eggs

1 c. milk

1 c. all-purpose flour

Pinch of salt

1 Tbsp. granulated sugar

1 tsp. pure vanilla extract

Dash of cinnamon

1/3 stick unsalted butter

Preheat your oven to 425°F. Preferably in a blender, mix eggs, milk, flour, salt, sugar, vanilla extract, and cinnamon. The better blended it is, the fluffier your final product will be. In the meantime, place your dish in the oven with the 1/3 stick of butter. You can either use a 9x13" casserole dish or 12" cast iron high-sided pan, which is what Lenny prefers. Check your pan frequently, as you are wanting the butter melt and slightly brown. Once the pan is ready, pull it from the oven carefully with a hot pad or oven mitt. Pour your prepared batter quickly into the pan and immediately return it to the oven. Bake it for approximately 20-25 minutes or until puffed and golden brown. When it is cooked, pull it from the oven and serve immediately. Dutch Babies are delicious served with powdered sugar, maple syrup, fresh berries, yogurt, bananas, bacon, honey, jam, and anything else you would include with pancakes. **Serves 4**

Silver Dollar Pancakes

1 c. all-purpose flour

1 Tbsp. baking Powder

½ tsp. salt

2. Tbsp. granulated sugar

1 c. milk

2 Tbsp. of melted butter

1 egg

Warm up a griddle or large nonstick pan on medium heat. Mix all above ingredients. Lightly grease your griddle with butter or an oil of choice. Once the batter is done, we like to pour it into a wide mouth squeeze bottle. This makes it much easier to create the smaller sized pancakes seen above in the photo or larger depending on whether you are a human or a lizard (although you should never feed your lizard pancakes, and even Chef Lenny knows that). Once your batter has been squirted onto the griddle, watch for bubbles! The rule of thumb is ten bubbles = time to flip! You know that your pancakes are done with they are fluffy and golden brown. Top with the ingredients in the previous Dutch Baby recipe. **Serves 4**

Big Ole' Blueberry Muffins

½ c. softened butter

1 ¼ c. granulated sugar

2 eggs

1 tsp. pure vanilla extract

2 c. all-purpose flour

½ tsp. salt

2 tsp. baking powder

½ c. milk

2 c. blueberries (fresh preferred but frozen is fine if they are thawed)

3 tsp. turbinado sugar (to sprinkle on top of muffins right before baking)

Blueberry Muffin Instructions

Preheat oven to 400° F. Mix the butter and sugar till light and fluffy. Add the eggs, one at a time, mixing well after each addition. Add the vanilla extract. Mix the dry ingredients together (flour, salt & baking powder) in a separate bowl. Slowly add the dry ingredients to the wet ingredients a little at a time alternating with the milk. Gently fold in the berries.

Grease a 6-cup large muffin tin or line a standard 12-cup muffin tin with liners. Fill each cup 2/3 of the way full of the batter. Sprinkle the remaining sugar over the tops of the uncooked muffins.

Now *reduce* the oven temperature to 375° and bake for approximately 30-35 minutes, or until an inserted toothpick comes out clean.

Once the muffins are done, immediately remove them from the tins. This prevents them from continuing to bake and get "tough" on the bottom or burnt.

The muffins can be stored at room temperature for 1 day. **Serves 6**

Best Belgian Waffles

2 c. flour

4 tsp. baking powder

½ tsp. Salt

¼ c. sugar

2 eggs

½ c. corn oil

2 c. almond milk

1 tsp. vanilla

Heat up waffle iron. Ours has a Belgian Waffle setting, so we use that. Place all wet ingredients into a blender. Turn on low speed and slowly add dry ingredients. Blend up until well combined. Pour about ¼ to 1/3 cup of batter into each waffle square if yours has multiple zones. Cook till golden brown (around 4 minutes). Serve with berries, whipped cream, syrup, honey, powdered sugar, bananas, peanut butter, etc.! The options are endless. **Serves 4**

TO AVOID SMUDGING, USE PERMENANT MARKER AND ALLOW ADEQUATE TIME TO DRY INK.

RECIPE:_____

INGREDIENTS:_____

INSTRUCTIONS:_____

TO AVOID SMUDGING, USE PERMENANT MARKER AND ALLOW ADEQUATE TIME TO DRY INK.

RECIPE:_____

INGREDIENTS:_____

INSTRUCTIONS:_____

TO AVOID SMUDGING, USE PERMENANT MARKER AND ALLOW ADEQUATE TIME TO DRY INK.

RECIPE:_____

INGREDIENTS:_____

_____
_____
_____
_____
_____
_____
_____

INSTRUCTIONS:_____

_____
_____
_____
_____
_____
_____
_____
_____
_____
_____
_____
_____

TO AVOID SMUDGING, USE PERMENANT MARKER AND ALLOW ADEQUATE TIME TO
DRY INK.

RECIPE:_____

INGREDIENTS:_____

_____
_____
_____
_____
_____
_____
_____

INSTRUCTIONS:_____

_____
_____
_____
_____
_____
_____
_____
_____
_____
_____
_____
_____
_____
_____

TO AVOID SMUDGING, USE PERMENANT MARKER AND ALLOW ADEQUATE TIME TO DRY INK.

RECIPE:_____

INGREDIENTS:_____

_____
_____
_____
_____
_____
_____
_____

INSTRUCTIONS:_____

_____
_____
_____
_____
_____
_____
_____
_____
_____
_____
_____
_____
_____

TO AVOID SMUDGING, USE PERMENANT MARKER AND ALLOW ADEQUATE TIME TO
DRY INK.

RECIPE:_____

INGREDIENTS:_____

_____
_____
_____
_____
_____
_____
_____

INSTRUCTIONS:_____

_____
_____
_____
_____
_____
_____
_____
_____
_____
_____
_____
_____
_____
_____

TO AVOID SMUDGING, USE PERMENANT MARKER AND ALLOW ADEQUATE TIME TO
DRY INK.

RECIPE:_____

INGREDIENTS:_____

INSTRUCTIONS:_____

TO AVOID SMUDGING, USE PERMENANT MARKER AND ALLOW ADEQUATE TIME TO DRY INK.

RECIPE: _____

INGREDIENTS: _____

_____
_____
_____
_____
_____
_____

INSTRUCTIONS: _____

_____
_____
_____
_____
_____
_____
_____
_____
_____
_____
_____
_____

TO AVOID SMUDGING, USE PERMENANT MARKER AND ALLOW ADEQUATE TIME TO DRY INK.

RECIPE:_____

INGREDIENTS:_____

_____
_____
_____
_____
_____
_____
_____

INSTRUCTIONS:_____

_____
_____
_____
_____
_____
_____
_____
_____
_____
_____
_____
_____
_____

TO AVOID SMUDGING, USE PERMENANT MARKER AND ALLOW ADEQUATE TIME TO DRY INK.

RECIPE: _____

INGREDIENTS: _____

_____
_____
_____
_____
_____
_____
_____

INSTRUCTIONS: _____

_____
_____
_____
_____
_____
_____
_____
_____
_____
_____
_____
_____
_____

It is Soup Day

Chicken & Wild Rice Soup

2 Tbsp. olive oil

1 c. diced celery

1 c. diced carrots

1 large diced yellow onion

3 minced garlic cloves

2 chicken breasts diced

1 c. cooked brown rice

¼ c. uncooked wild rice

4 c. chicken broth

2 c. water

1 Tbsp. salt

1 tsp. Herbs de Provence

Pepper to taste

Heat oil in a large Dutch oven on medium. Add the celery, carrots, onion, and garlic. Cook until softened. Add diced chicken breast and stir. Cook the veggies and chicken together for 5 minutes. Add broth and water. Bring to simmer. Add both kinds of rice, salt, Herbs de Provence, and pepper. Simmer for 30 minutes. Add more salt and pepper as needed.

Serves 8

Ma's Split Pea Soup

2 Tbsp. olive oil

1 large white onion

5 large carrots

2 c. chopped celery

1 tsp. salt

1 tsp. black pepper

2 c. dried split peas

2 Tbsp. Better Than
Bouillon (chicken)

6 c. water

1 bay leaf

1 Tbsp. fresh tarragon

Parsley for garnish

Heat oil in a cast iron Dutch oven on medium heat. Dice onion, carrot, and celery and add to pot. Sprinkle with salt and pepper. Sauté till veggies are wilted and onion is lightly browned. Pour in the water and add the peas. Bring to a boil. Lower the heat and add the bay leaf, chicken bouillon, and tarragon. Simmer on low for 30 minutes or until peas have softened. Remove the bay leaf. Add more salt and pepper as needed. Sprinkle the chopped parsley for garnish and serve with a crusty bread. Enjoy hot or cold. **Serves 6**

Chickpea Coconut Curry

1 Tbsp. oil

1 diced large onion

3 minced cloves garlic

1 minced finger ginger

1 Tbsp. garam marsala

¼ tsp. ground turmeric

¼ tsp. black pepper

¼ tsp. cayenne pepper

1 can diced tomatoes

1 14 oz. can coconut milk

1 16 oz. can chickpeas

2 Tbsp. lime juice

Chopped cilantro to serve

In a large Dutch oven, heat oil on medium, add the onion with a pinch of salt. Cook and stir till lightly browned. Add garlic and ginger, garam marsala, turmeric, peppers, and another pinch of salt. Cook till fragrant. Add the tomatoes to the pan and stir occasionally, till they break down and dry slightly. Stir in coconut milk and chickpeas. Bring to boil, then reduce heat to medium-low. Simmer for 10 minutes, and then stir in lime juice. Season with salt and pepper to taste. Serve hot or cold over rice and garnish with cilantro. **Serves 4**

Green Chili

1 lb. ground beef (90/10)

1 diced onion

3 chopped celery stalks

1 diced bell pepper

3 minced cloves garlic

2 diced jalapeños

2 cubed potatoes

1 can diced green chilis

1 can corn (rinsed)

1 can black beans (rinsed)

1 can Mexican tomatoes

3 Tbsp. cumin

1 Tbsp. taco seasoning

1 Tbsp. salt

In a large Dutch oven or soup pot, brown the beef with the garlic. Add the cumin, salt, onion, celery, jalapeños, taco seasoning, and sauté with the beef / garlic mixture for 2 minutes. Add the bell pepper, green chilis, potatoes, tomatoes, & water (just to cover all the ingredients). Simmer until potatoes soften. Finally add the corn and beans. Fill individual bowls and top with avocado, shredded cheese, fresh cilantro, sour cream, salsa, blue corn chips or whatever else you enjoy with your tacos! **Serves 6**

Corn Chowder

2 Tbsp. butter

8 strips of bacon (sliced)

1 large diced onion

2 large diced carrots

5 ribs celery

2 c. diced red potatoes

2 cans creamed corn

1 can sweet corn

1 bay leaf

½ Tbsp. fresh thyme

Pinch red pepper flakes

Salt and pepper to taste

1 c. of half and half

Chicken broth as needed (about 3 c.)

In a large Dutch oven or soup pot on medium heat, add the butter and melt. Then add the bacon and stir to cook. When the bacon is browned, add the onion, celery, and carrots to the pot. Sauté until the onions are translucent. Now add the corn, potatoes, half and half, and spices. Pour in chicken broth to just cover the mixture. Bring to a light simmer and cook 15-20 minutes till the potatoes have softened. If you want a thicker chowder, you can add ¼ cup of flour or 1 Tbsp of corn starch while you are sautéing the veggies. **Serves 6-8**

TO AVOID SMUDGING, USE PERMENANT MARKER AND ALLOW ADEQUATE TIME TO DRY INK.

RECIPE:_____

INGREDIENTS:_____

_____
_____
_____
_____
_____
_____
_____

INSTRUCTIONS:_____

_____
_____
_____
_____
_____
_____
_____
_____
_____
_____
_____
_____
_____

TO AVOID SMUDGING, USE PERMENANT MARKER AND ALLOW ADEQUATE TIME TO
DRY INK.

RECIPE:_____

INGREDIENTS:_____
_____
_____
_____
_____
_____
_____
_____

INSTRUCTIONS:_____
_____
_____
_____
_____
_____
_____
_____
_____
_____
_____
_____
_____
_____

TO AVOID SMUDGING, USE PERMENANT MARKER AND ALLOW ADEQUATE TIME TO DRY INK.

RECIPE:_____

INGREDIENTS:_____

_____
_____
_____
_____
_____
_____
_____

INSTRUCTIONS:_____

_____
_____
_____
_____
_____
_____
_____
_____
_____
_____
_____

TO AVOID SMUDGING, USE PERMENANT MARKER AND ALLOW ADEQUATE TIME TO
DRY INK.

RECIPE: _____

INGREDIENTS: _____

INSTRUCTIONS: _____

TO AVOID SMUDGING, USE PERMENANT MARKER AND ALLOW ADEQUATE TIME TO
DRY INK.

RECIPE: _____

INGREDIENTS: _____

_____
_____
_____
_____
_____
_____
_____

INSTRUCTIONS: _____

_____
_____
_____
_____
_____
_____
_____
_____
_____
_____
_____
_____
_____
_____

TO AVOID SMUDGING, USE PERMENANT MARKER AND ALLOW ADEQUATE TIME TO DRY INK.

RECIPE:_____

INGREDIENTS:_____

_____
_____
_____
_____
_____
_____
_____

INSTRUCTIONS:_____

_____
_____
_____
_____
_____
_____
_____
_____
_____
_____
_____
_____
_____
_____

TO AVOID SMUDGING, USE PERMENANT MARKER AND ALLOW ADEQUATE TIME TO DRY INK.

RECIPE: _____

INGREDIENTS: _____

_____
_____
_____
_____
_____
_____
_____

INSTRUCTIONS: _____

_____
_____
_____
_____
_____
_____
_____
_____
_____
_____
_____
_____
_____

TO AVOID SMUDGING, USE PERMENANT MARKER AND ALLOW ADEQUATE TIME TO DRY INK.

RECIPE:_____

INGREDIENTS:_____

_____
_____
_____
_____
_____
_____
_____

INSTRUCTIONS:_____

_____
_____
_____
_____
_____
_____
_____
_____
_____
_____
_____
_____
_____

TO AVOID SMUDGING, USE PERMENANT MARKER AND ALLOW ADEQUATE TIME TO
DRY INK.

RECIPE:_____

INGREDIENTS:_____

_____
_____
_____
_____
_____
_____
_____

INSTRUCTIONS:_____

_____
_____
_____
_____
_____
_____
_____
_____
_____
_____
_____
_____

TO AVOID SMUDGING, USE PERMENANT MARKER AND ALLOW ADEQUATE TIME TO
DRY INK.

RECIPE:_____

INGREDIENTS:_____

INSTRUCTIONS:_____

Fancy Finger Foods

Laugenbrezel / Soft German Pretzels

Pretzel Dough

3 c. all-purpose flour

1 Tbsp. active dry yeast

1 tsp. granulated sugar

2 Tbsp. softened butter

1 1/3 c. water

¼ tsp. salt

Water Bath

3 Tbsp. baking soda

3 c. water

For Tops

2 Tbsp. butter, melted

1 Tbsp. Kosher Salt

Laugenbrezel Instructions

In a large bowl stir together 1 cup flour, yeast, sugar, 2 Tbsp butter, and 1 1/3 cup of water. Let this sit until the yeast reaction gets foamy (about 15 minutes). Add the salt and gradually stir in the remaining flour until dough forms and can be taken out of the bowl and kneaded on the countertop or in a stand mixer. Knead by hand or with mixer for 8 – 10 minutes till the dough is smooth and elastic. Add flour as needed one tablespoon at a time.

Divide your dough in 6 to 8 pieces and let them rest for 5 minutes. Roll out one piece at a time into a rope about 15 inches long. Loop and twist into a pretzel shape. Set on a baking sheet lined with parchment paper (or a baking mat) while you continue rolling out the other portions.

Preheat the oven to 450°F. Bring the remaining 3 cups of water to a boil in a large pot. Add the baking soda to the boiling water. Remove from the heat. Dip pretzels in the water for 45 seconds, flipping them halfway to ensure that the whole piece gets soaked. Place the soaked pretzel back on the baking sheet. Continue with each portion. When they are all finished soaking, brush the tops with melted butter and sprinkle with kosher salt.

Bake in the oven until golden brown, for about 8 to 10 minutes.

We like to dip our pretzels in a cheese sauce or stone-ground mustard! **Serves 6 - 8**

Tortilla Pizza Bites

3 large tortillas

1 jar pasta or pizza sauce

1 c. shredded mozzarella cheese

1 package turkey pepperonis

1 can sliced black olives

Nonstick cooking spray

Preheat the oven to 350°F. Spray a 12-count muffin tin with nonstick cooking spray. Cut twelve 3 ½ inch circles out of the tortillas. I find that a wide-mouth mason jar ring works best for this project! Push the tortilla rounds into the muffin tin cups leaving a bit of space between the bottom of the tortilla tin (this prevents the bottom from sticking). Place 1 tablespoon of sauce in the tortilla cup. Add a pinch of mozzarella. Add toppings. We like to use turkey pepperoni and black olives, but the possibilities are endless. Add another pinch of mozzarella. When all the tins are filled, bake in the preheated oven till the cheese is melted on top (approximately 10 minutes). Let cool slightly before removing them from the tin. A butter knife is a great way to help pop them out! **Serves 3**

Mini Quiche Bites

2 pie crusts

1 lb. bacon cut into strips

1 large yellow onion

1 c. shredded cheese (cheddar, swiss or gruyere)

4 large eggs

1 ¼ c. milk

1 tsp. Dijon mustard

¼ tsp. salt

¼ tsp. fresh cracked pepper

Pinch of thyme

Preheat Oven to 375°. Grease a standard sized muffin tin. Cut pie crust with a large-mouth mason jar ring and push into muffin tin. Sauté onion and bacon together until the onion turns translucent. In a bowl, add eggs, cheese, milk, mustard, salt, pepper, and thyme. Mix until well incorporated. Scoop bacon and onion evenly into each pie cup. Pour egg mixture just up to the edge of the sides of the pie crust. Bake for 20 to 25 minutes or until the centers are puffed and lightly browned. Carefully loosen edges and pop out and cool on a cooling rack. Enjoy warm. **Serves 4**

TO AVOID SMUDGING, USE PERMENANT MARKER AND ALLOW ADEQUATE TIME TO
DRY INK.

RECIPE:_____

INGREDIENTS:_____

_____
_____
_____
_____
_____
_____

INSTRUCTIONS:_____

_____
_____
_____
_____
_____
_____
_____
_____
_____
_____
_____

TO AVOID SMUDGING, USE PERMENANT MARKER AND ALLOW ADEQUATE TIME TO DRY INK.

RECIPE: _____

INGREDIENTS: _____

_____
_____
_____
_____
_____
_____
_____

INSTRUCTIONS: _____

_____
_____
_____
_____
_____
_____
_____
_____
_____
_____
_____
_____
_____

TO AVOID SMUDGING, USE PERMENANT MARKER AND ALLOW ADEQUATE TIME TO
DRY INK.

RECIPE:_____

INGREDIENTS:_____

_____
_____
_____
_____
_____
_____
_____

INSTRUCTIONS:_____

_____
_____
_____
_____
_____
_____
_____
_____
_____
_____
_____
_____

TO AVOID SMUDGING, USE PERMENANT MARKER AND ALLOW ADEQUATE TIME TO
DRY INK.

RECIPE:_____

INGREDIENTS:_____
_____
_____
_____
_____
_____
_____

INSTRUCTIONS:_____
_____
_____
_____
_____
_____
_____
_____
_____
_____
_____
_____
_____

TO AVOID SMUDGING, USE PERMENANT MARKER AND ALLOW ADEQUATE TIME TO DRY INK.

RECIPE: _____

INGREDIENTS: _____

_____
_____
_____
_____
_____
_____
_____

INSTRUCTIONS: _____

_____
_____
_____
_____
_____
_____
_____
_____
_____
_____
_____
_____
_____

TO AVOID SMUDGING, USE PERMENANT MARKER AND ALLOW ADEQUATE TIME TO DRY INK.

RECIPE:_____

INGREDIENTS:_____
_____
_____
_____
_____
_____
_____
_____

INSTRUCTIONS:_____
_____
_____
_____
_____
_____
_____
_____
_____
_____
_____
_____
_____
_____
_____

TO AVOID SMUDGING, USE PERMENANT MARKER AND ALLOW ADEQUATE TIME TO DRY INK.

RECIPE:_____

INGREDIENTS:_____

_____
_____
_____
_____
_____
_____
_____

INSTRUCTIONS:_____

_____
_____
_____
_____
_____
_____
_____
_____
_____
_____
_____
_____
_____

TO AVOID SMUDGING, USE PERMENANT MARKER AND ALLOW ADEQUATE TIME TO DRY INK.

RECIPE:_____

INGREDIENTS:_____

_____
_____
_____
_____
_____
_____
_____
_____

INSTRUCTIONS:_____

_____
_____
_____
_____
_____
_____
_____
_____
_____
_____
_____
_____
_____
_____

TO AVOID SMUDGING, USE PERMENANT MARKER AND ALLOW ADEQUATE TIME TO DRY INK.

RECIPE: _____

INGREDIENTS: _____

INSTRUCTIONS: _____

TO AVOID SMUDGING, USE PERMENANT MARKER AND ALLOW ADEQUATE TIME TO DRY INK.

RECIPE:_____

INGREDIENTS:_____

_____
_____
_____
_____
_____
_____
_____

INSTRUCTIONS:_____

_____
_____
_____
_____
_____
_____
_____
_____
_____
_____
_____
_____

Playing with Dough

Hand Tossed Pizza Dough

15g yeast

500g Italian pizza flour

10g salt

50g olive oil

320g water

Add all the above ingredient to a mixing bowl and combine. Knead with a high-powered mixer or by hand for a minimum of 10 minutes. You want this to dough to be silky and elastic. Cover and let it rest for a minimum of 1 hour, but ideally overnight in the fridge to develop a better flavor and crispier crust.

When the dough is ready, preheat the oven to 450°F (or hotter, if your oven will allow). Turn dough out onto floured surface and divide into three even pieces. Work the dough into a rough circle about 10-12 inches in diameter. Repeat with the other two pieces of dough. Once all the dough pieces are shaped, you are ready to add your toppings of choice! Lenny loves to keep it simple with red sauce, black olives, turkey pepperoni, mozzarella cheese and fresh basil, but the sky's the limit! He always weighs out his ingredients when he works with artisanal dough recipes. **Serves 3**

Pie & Quiche Crust

2 ½ c. flour

1 tsp. salt

1 tsp. sugar

1 c. cold butter (cut into cubes)

½ c. ice water (give or take)

Pulse flour, salt, and sugar together in a food processor. Add the butter piece by piece and pulse till the mixture resembles sand. Slowly add the ice water, a bit at a time, till the dough just comes together. Form into a ball, wrap in plastic wrap for at least 30 minutes till ready for use. This works for BOTH pie and quiche.
Yield 2 Crusts

Cinnamon Rolls

Dough

4 ½ tsp. active dry yeast

1 c. lukewarm water

1 tsp. sugar

6 Tbsp. vegetable shortening

1 c. sugar

8-10 c. flour

2 c. hot water

2 eggs (beaten)

1 tsp. salt

1 stick soft butter

1 ½ c. brown Sugar

Cinnamon (1/2 Tbsp. roughly)

Unflavored dental floss

Cream Cheese Frosting

8 oz. cream cheese (room temp), 3 ½ c. powdered sugar, 1 tsp. vanilla extract, 3 Tbsp. corn oil, ½ tsp salt

Cinnamon Roll Instructions

In a small bowl add yeast and lukewarm water. Allow it to set for 5 minutes or until foamy. In the bowl of a stand mixer, add shortening, sugar, salt, 2 cups hot water and beat for 30 seconds using the beater blade. Switch out to the dough hook blade and add in 2 cups of flour, yeast/water mix and beaten eggs. Mix until smooth. Gradually add in the rest of the flour, beating until it comes together. Knead until silky and smooth, around 10 minutes or so. Cover bowl and place in a warm, draft-free area to rise for 30 minutes.

Preheat oven to 350°

Once the dough has risen, divide in half. Roll out one half into a rough rectangular shape about 1/8 inch thick. Slather on softened butter, sprinkle with brown sugar and dust on cinnamon. Starting on the SHORT end, roll it up Jelly Roll style. Cut into 8 equal pieces using unflavored dental floss or a serrated knife. Place your individual rolls into a greased 9x13, 5.5 QT Dutch oven, cookie sheet, or other large baking dish. Repeat with the other half of the dough. Once all cinnamon rolls are in their respective places, cover and let them rise again till they have doubled in size.

Bake at 350° for 20 minutes (30 minutes if using cast iron). The tops should be a golden brown. Let cool.

While the Cinnamon Rolls are cooling, make the frosting! Beat cream cheese and oil till fluffy. Then beat in sugar, vanilla, and salt until exceptionally smooth and spreadable. Dollop onto warm cinnamon rolls so it melts into all the crevasses. Enjoy warm or room temperature. **Serves 8 to 16**

Dutch Oven Bread

2 c. water

4 c. flour

2 ¼ tsp. active dry yeast

10 g. salt

¼ to 1/2 c. starter (optional)

Add all the ingredients to a mixer bowl or large bowl. Mix on high or by hand till it all comes together. We use a high-protein bread flour and the process takes about 10 to 15 minutes. Cover bowl and let rise for 2 hours or until doubled in size. Punch it down. Cover it again and let it rise till doubled in size. Preheat your oven to 450° and put your empty Dutch oven in to heat up as well. After the bread has risen, shape into a ball and let it rest on the counter with a tea towel over it for 30 minutes (dusting your loaf and countertop with flour will prevent it from sticking to the surface). Score with a sharp blade. Plop it in the hot Dutch oven (a cookie sheet will also work). Bake for 30 minutes with the lid ON. After 30 minutes, remove the lid and bake for an additional 15 to 25 minutes. Remove when the top of the loaf is a nice golden brown. Let completely cool before cutting into as it will still be baking on the inside! **Yields 1 loaf**

TO AVOID SMUDGING, USE PERMENANT MARKER AND ALLOW ADEQUATE TIME TO DRY INK.

RECIPE: _____

INGREDIENTS: _____

_____
_____
_____
_____
_____
_____
_____

INSTRUCTIONS: _____

_____
_____
_____
_____
_____
_____
_____
_____
_____
_____
_____
_____
_____

TO AVOID SMUDGING, USE PERMENANT MARKER AND ALLOW ADEQUATE TIME TO DRY INK.

RECIPE:_____

INGREDIENTS:_____

INSTRUCTIONS:_____

TO AVOID SMUDGING, USE PERMENANT MARKER AND ALLOW ADEQUATE TIME TO
DRY INK.

RECIPE:_____

INGREDIENTS:_____

_____
_____
_____
_____
_____
_____
_____

INSTRUCTIONS:_____

_____
_____
_____
_____
_____
_____
_____
_____
_____
_____
_____
_____

TO AVOID SMUDGING, USE PERMENANT MARKER AND ALLOW ADEQUATE TIME TO
DRY INK.

RECIPE: _____

INGREDIENTS: _____

_____
_____
_____
_____
_____
_____
_____
_____

INSTRUCTIONS: _____

_____
_____
_____
_____
_____
_____
_____
_____
_____
_____
_____
_____
_____
_____

TO AVOID SMUDGING, USE PERMENANT MARKER AND ALLOW ADEQUATE TIME TO
DRY INK.

RECIPE: _____

INGREDIENTS: _____

_____
_____
_____
_____
_____
_____
_____

INSTRUCTIONS: _____

_____
_____
_____
_____
_____
_____
_____
_____
_____
_____
_____
_____
_____

TO AVOID SMUDGING, USE PERMENANT MARKER AND ALLOW ADEQUATE TIME TO DRY INK.

RECIPE: _____

INGREDIENTS: _____

_____
_____
_____
_____
_____
_____
_____

INSTRUCTIONS: _____

_____
_____
_____
_____
_____
_____
_____
_____
_____
_____
_____

TO AVOID SMUDGING, USE PERMENANT MARKER AND ALLOW ADEQUATE TIME TO DRY INK.

RECIPE: _____

INGREDIENTS: _____

_____
_____
_____
_____
_____
_____
_____

INSTRUCTIONS: _____

_____
_____
_____
_____
_____
_____
_____
_____
_____
_____
_____
_____
_____

TO AVOID SMUDGING, USE PERMENANT MARKER AND ALLOW ADEQUATE TIME TO DRY INK.

RECIPE:_____

INGREDIENTS:_____

_____
_____
_____
_____
_____
_____

INSTRUCTIONS:_____

_____
_____
_____
_____
_____
_____
_____
_____
_____
_____
_____
_____
_____

TO AVOID SMUDGING, USE PERMENANT MARKER AND ALLOW ADEQUATE TIME TO DRY INK.

RECIPE:_____

INGREDIENTS:_____

_____
_____
_____
_____
_____
_____
_____

INSTRUCTIONS:_____

_____
_____
_____
_____
_____
_____
_____
_____
_____
_____
_____
_____

TO AVOID SMUDGING, USE PERMENANT MARKER AND ALLOW ADEQUATE TIME TO DRY INK.

RECIPE:_____

INGREDIENTS:_____

_____
_____
_____
_____
_____
_____
_____

INSTRUCTIONS:_____

_____
_____
_____
_____
_____
_____
_____
_____
_____
_____
_____
_____
_____
_____

Impressive Entrees

Chicken Pot Pie

3 Tbsp. butter

1 large onion diced

3 celery stalks diced

2 medium carrots diced

½ c. frozen peas

½ c. frozen corn

2 Tbsp. corn starch
(mixed in a bit of water)

2 cups chicken broth

1 lb. of diced chicken

1 unbaked pie crust or 1
sheet puff pastry

1 egg beaten for egg wash

Chicken Pot Pie Instructions

In a large oven-safe, high-sided skillet, melt butter over medium-high heat. Add onion, celery, and carrots. Cook until onion is translucent, (about 4 minutes). Toss in the chicken and stir to cook. When it is completely cooked, add the peas, corn, and stir to heat for about 2 minutes. Pour in the corn starch slurry or replace with 4 tablespoons of all-purpose flour and stir to incorporate. Gradually add the broth, stirring constantly while it thickens. Once it begins to boil, turn it down and allow it to simmer for 5 minutes. Season with salt and pepper. Scoop mixture into individual ramekins and top with the pie crust, make an "X" on each to allow for steam to release. Alternatively, you can keep it all in the large oven-safe skillet and top with a sheet of puff pastry. Brush with egg wash and bake for 25-30 minutes or until tops are puffed and golden brown. **Serves 6**

Loaded Baked Potato

4 **BIG** Russet potatoes

olive oil

salt

Preheat your oven to 450°F. Poke your potatoes all over with a fork. This helps release steam while they are cooking. Rub oil all over them! Place them on top of a foil lined cookie sheet. Salt the skin. Bake for about 1 hour. You can reach in and squeeze them with an oven mitt to check if they are done. If they are not quite soft enough, keep them in the oven and continue baking and checking every 5 minutes or so. When they are baked, slice across the top, squeeze open on both opposing ends and fluff with a fork! Add your favorite toppings.

Lenny likes to add butter, salt, pepper, sour cream, cheddar cheese, turkey bacon and green onions! **Serves 4**

Turkey Tacos

1 Tbsp. olive oil

1 lb. ground turkey

1 can black beans

1 can fire roasted tomaotes

1 package taco seasoning

Toppings:

Cabbage slaw

Rice

Sour cream

Salsa

Avocado

Cheese

In a large skillet, heat olive oil on medium heat, add ground turkey and cook until browned. At this point, add the taco seasoning packet, or make your own seasoning! It's very simple and comes in handy for other dishes! Stir it around until it is fully incorporated. Drain black beans and tomatoes together in the same colander. Add to turkey mixture. Add ½ cup water to the skillet and let simmer on low for about 10 minutes or until the sauce has thickened slightly and it is heated through. Prepare with corn or flour tortillas and add the toppings of your choice! **Serves 4**

Fried Rice

3 Tbsp. butter (divided)

3 eggs

2 carrots diced

1 onion diced

½ c. frozen peas

4 cloves garlic minced

Salt & pepper to taste

¼ c. green onions chopped

4 Tbsp. soy sauce

4 c. of cooked and cooled rice

2 tsp. of sesame oil

1 Tbsp. black sesame seeds

In a large high-sided skillet, melt 1 Tbsp. of butter on medium-high heat. Add the eggs and scramble, set aside. Add the other two tablespoons of butter to the skillet, melt and then add the carrots, diced onion, garlic, salt, and pepper. Cook until the onion begins to turn translucent. Add the rice, green onions, soy sauce, and scrambled eggs. Cook, mixing well until veggies are slightly browned and rice is reheated (about 5 minutes). Turn off the heat, add the sesame oil and black sesame seeds and stir to incorporate. **Serves 4 to 6**

Curried Chicken Salad Wraps

3-4 10oz cans chicken in water (drained)

4 celery ribs diced

1 medium onion diced

½ c. mayonnaise

1 Tbsp. Dijon mustard

1 tsp. curry powder

¼ tsp. ground turmeric

Salt & pepper to taste

Pinch of cayenne

1 head Romaine lettuce

Spinach wraps

Drain chicken and place into a medium mixing bowl. Add the rest of the ingredients. Stir till it is all well combined. Let sit in the fridge for 30 minutes to allow the flavors to combine. Place your wrap on a cutting board and put a romaine leaf in the middle. Scoop out about ½ cup of chicken mixture and place it on top of the romaine lettuce. Starting on the wrap edge closest to you, roll forward halfway, fold the sides in, and complete the roll, creating a burrito. Slice in half diagonally and serve. We enjoy ours with salad, mac 'n cheese or sweet potato fries. **Serves 6**

Turkey Stroganoff

1 lb. ground turkey

1 tsp. salt

½ tsp. ground pepper

4 Tbsp. butter

1 large white onion

3 garlic cloves

8 oz. mushrooms

2 Tbsp. all-purpose flour

1 ½ c. beef broth

1 Tbsp. Worcestershire

1 Tbsp. Dijon mustard

Squeeze of lemon

1 tsp. fresh thyme

¾ c. sour cream

9 oz. penne noodles

Chopped parsley & green onions for garnish

Turkey Stroganoff Instructions

Heat one Tbsp. butter in a large high-sided skillet on medium-high heat. Add the ground turkey and brown. While the turkey is browning, add the salt and pepper. When the turkey is completely cooked, add another Tbsp. butter, onion, garlic, and the mushrooms. Cook for 4 to 5 minutes until the onions are lightly caramelized.

Reduce the heat to medium-low and add the final 2 tablespoons of butter. When that has melted, sprinkle the flour evenly around the pan and stir to coat the mixture. Once incorporated, slowly pour in the broth, stirring constantly. Let the mixture come to a bubble, then stir in Worcestershire, Dijon mustard, thyme, lemon juice and sour cream.

Reduce the heat again to low and allow the sauce to cook for an additional 5 minutes. This is a great time to start cooking your pasta-of-choice according to the package's directions. The sauce will thicken as it sits.

Once the pasta is cooked, add to bowls and ladle the Stroganoff Sauce on top. Garnish with green onions and/or parsley. **Serves 4**

Boeuf Bourguignon

½ lb. bacon

3 ½ Tbsp. olive oil

3 lb. chuck beef roast (1 to 2-inch chunks)

4 large carrots (sliced)

2 large white onions (sliced or diced)

1 pinch sea salt

2 Tbsp. flour

1 bottle red wine

1 Tbsp. tomato paste

5 cloves garlic crushed or diced

1 Tbsp. fresh thyme

2 bay leaves

10 pearl onions

4 Tbsp. butter

1 Tbsp. fresh parsley

1 lb. mushrooms sliced

Boeuf Bourguignon Instructions

Preheat oven to 425°F. On the stovetop, heat a large Dutch oven (we use a 13.25 QT oven for this project) on medium-high heat. Cut the bacon into small strips and place in hot pan. When browned, remove from pan, and set aside. Add beef chunks to hot pan. Brown evenly on all sides. You may need to do this in stages, depending on the size of your Dutch oven. If you do not give the beef enough space, it will just get foamy rather than brown the beef evenly. When the beef is browned on all sides, remove from the pan and set aside with the bacon. Add the sliced carrots and onions to the hot pan and sauté in the fat till they are browned. Add the beef and bacon back to the hot pot, season with salt and pepper, toss with flour, stir, sprinkle with a bit more flour and place into the hot oven for 5 minutes.

Remove from oven, stir it around and put it back in for 4 minutes. At this point, reduce the oven temperature to 325°F. Now, pour in the bottle of wine, beef stock and tablespoon of tomato paste. Stir it around until incorporated. Add crushed garlic, thyme, parsley, bay leaves, pearl onions, butter and mushrooms. Sprinkle in a bit of salt and pepper (1/4 tsp. or so). Bring to a simmer and then place the Dutch oven back into the oven and cook for 5 hours at 325°F.

When the Boeuf Bourguignon has cooked for 5 hours, drain the stew through a colander into another pot or bowl. Pour the beef and veggies back into the Dutch oven. Simmer the broth separately for approximately 5 minutes, as to slightly reduce. Pour the reduced sauce over the beef and veggies and simmer for an additional 5 minutes.

Serve in a bowl, with a crusty bread and shaved parmesan. **Serves 4 to 6**

Sweet & Spicy Salmon

1 3lb. whole fresh salmon fillet

3 Tbsp. softened butter

½ c. of brown sugar

¼ tsp. chipotle powder

¼ tsp. granulated garlic

Salt & pepper

Preheat oven to 475°F. Line a sheet pan with parchment paper or foil. Place whole fillet onto parchment paper. Smear the softened butter all over the salmon fillet. Rub on brown sugar, trying to evenly coat entire fillet. Sprinkle chipotle and granulated garlic across the whole fish and then do the same with the salt and pepper. Bake for 20 to 25 minutes. **Serves 4**

RECIPE: _____

INGREDIENTS: _____

_____
_____
_____
_____
_____
_____
_____

INSTRUCTIONS: _____

_____
_____
_____
_____
_____
_____
_____
_____
_____
_____
_____
_____
_____

TO AVOID SMUDGING, USE PERMENANT MARKER AND ALLOW ADEQUATE TIME TO DRY INK.

RECIPE:_____

INGREDIENTS:_____

_____
_____
_____
_____
_____
_____
_____

INSTRUCTIONS:_____

_____
_____
_____
_____
_____
_____
_____
_____
_____
_____
_____
_____
_____

TO AVOID SMUDGING, USE PERMENANT MARKER AND ALLOW ADEQUATE TIME TO
DRY INK.

RECIPE:_____

INGREDIENTS:_____

INSTRUCTIONS:_____

TO AVOID SMUDGING, USE PERMENANT MARKER AND ALLOW ADEQUATE TIME TO DRY INK.

RECIPE:_____

INGREDIENTS:_____

_____
_____
_____
_____
_____
_____
_____

INSTRUCTIONS:_____

_____
_____
_____
_____
_____
_____
_____
_____
_____
_____
_____
_____
_____
_____

TO AVOID SMUDGING, USE PERMENANT MARKER AND ALLOW ADEQUATE TIME TO DRY INK.

RECIPE: _____

INGREDIENTS: _____

INSTRUCTIONS: _____

TO AVOID SMUDGING, USE PERMENANT MARKER AND ALLOW ADEQUATE TIME TO DRY INK.

RECIPE:_____

INGREDIENTS:_____

_____
_____
_____
_____
_____
_____
_____

INSTRUCTIONS:_____

_____
_____
_____
_____
_____
_____
_____
_____
_____
_____
_____
_____
_____

TO AVOID SMUDGING, USE PERMENANT MARKER AND ALLOW ADEQUATE TIME TO
DRY INK.

RECIPE: _____

INGREDIENTS: _____

INSTRUCTIONS: _____

TO AVOID SMUDGING, USE PERMENANT MARKER AND ALLOW ADEQUATE TIME TO
DRY INK.

RECIPE: _____

INGREDIENTS: _____

_____
_____
_____
_____
_____
_____
_____
_____

INSTRUCTIONS: _____

_____
_____
_____
_____
_____
_____
_____
_____
_____
_____
_____
_____
_____
_____

TO AVOID SMUDGING, USE PERMENANT MARKER AND ALLOW ADEQUATE TIME TO
DRY INK.

RECIPE:_____

INGREDIENTS:_____

_____
_____
_____
_____
_____

INSTRUCTIONS:_____

_____
_____
_____
_____
_____
_____
_____
_____
_____

TO AVOID SMUDGING, USE PERMENANT MARKER AND ALLOW ADEQUATE TIME TO
DRY INK.

RECIPE: _____

INGREDIENTS: _____

_____
_____
_____
_____
_____
_____
_____

INSTRUCTIONS: _____

_____
_____
_____
_____
_____
_____
_____
_____
_____
_____
_____
_____

TO AVOID SMUDGING, USE PERMENANT MARKER AND ALLOW ADEQUATE TIME TO
DRY INK.

Dreamy Desserts

Ma's Famous Carrot Cake

3 c. grated raw carrot

2 c. all-purpose flour

2 tsp. baking powder

1 tsp. baking soda

4 eggs

1 tsp. salt

2 tsp. cinnamon

1 c. corn oil

1 c. white sugar

1 c. brown sugar

Frosting

16oz softened cream cheese

4 c. powdered sugar

1 tsp. vanilla extract

3 Tbsp. corn oil

¼ tsp. salt

Carrot Cake Instructions

Preheat the oven to 325°F. Cut parchment to fit the bottom of two 9" round cake pans or one 9x13" casserole pan. Grease the inside edges to help ease removal after baking. Grade carrots and place into a large bowl along with the eggs, salt, oil, and sugars. In a smaller bowl, add flour, baking powder, baking soda & cinnamon. While stirring, add the dry mixture to the wet mixture and stir until incorporated. Pour the completed mixture into the prepared pan(s) and bake for 40-45 minutes, or until an inserted toothpick comes out clean. Cool completely in pan.

Beat cream cheese and oil with a mixer on medium-high speed until light and fluffy, then set your mixer to low and gradually add the sugar, scraping the sides of the mixing bowl as needed. Add the vanilla and salt and continue beating until fluffy and smooth.

Frost the cake and enjoy! **Serves 8-10**

German Chocolate Cake Bites

1 box of brownie mix:

(baked and cooled in a 9x13" pan)

Chocolate Buttercream:

6 Tbsp. of unsalted butter softened

2 1/3 c. powdered sugar

¾ c. Dutch Process cocoa

1/3 c. whole milk

2 tsp. vanilla extract

¼ tsp. salt

Walnut pieces (for topping)

1 biscuit cutter 2-inch size

Smallest size star tip (for piping)

Make Brownies according to package directions. Make sure that you line the bottom of the pan with parchment paper. Since we will be cutting out rounds, this makes the removal process easier. Allow to completely cool before proceeding. When the brownies are cool, cut out with your biscuit cutter as many circles as possible. Make your buttercream: beat the butter until smooth, add the cocoa, sugar, and beat until combined. Slowly stream in milk and vanilla and then add the salt. Continue beating until well combined, about 3 minutes. Increase the speed to high and fluff for an additional two minutes. Using a tiny star piping tip, make a ring of individual stars around the edge of the brownie round. In the center, gently add walnut pieces for decoration. **Serves 4**

Brookies

1 box chocolate brownie Mix

1 package chocolate chip cookie dough

Preheat the oven to 350° F. This is our favorite "cheater" recipe and we find that it works best when the cookie dough is allowed time to warm up first. Line a 9x13" casserole dish with parchment paper. When the cookie dough is room temperature, press it evenly into the 9x13" dish. In a medium sized bowl, prepare the brownie mix as instructed on the packaging. Spread evenly on top of cookie layer in the dish. Bake for 35-40 minutes or until and inserted toothpick comes out clean. Cool completely in the dish, for about an hour. Cut into 4x5 rows and serve with vanilla ice cream and drizzled with hot caramel. **Serves 5 to 10**

Ma's Famous Blackberry Crisp

For Filling

6-8 c. fresh blackberries

½ tsp. vanilla

1 squirt of lemon juice

*1/2 tsp. Speculaaskruiden

1/3 c. all-purpose flour

¼ tsp. salt

½ c. sugar

For Topping

1 ½ c. rolled oats

1 c. all-purpose flour

¼ tsp. Speculaaskruiden

1 c. brown sugar

¼ tsp. salt

1 stick cold butter (cold)

*Speculaaskruiden is a traditional Dutch spice. Lenny loves to use it in place of cinnamon in many recipes because it tastes like the holidays. You can make your very own spice mix by combining the following: 4 tsp. cinnamon, 1 tsp. clove, 1 tsp. mace, 1/3 tsp. ginger, ¼ tsp. white pepper, ¼ tsp. cardamom, ¼ tsp. anise, ¼ tsp. nutmeg, ¼ tsp. coriander.

Blackberry Crisp Instructions

Preheat oven to 350°F. Add 6-8 cups of berries to a large mixing bowl (if using frozen berries, please allow ample time to thaw). Add vanilla, lemon juice, Speculaaskruiden, all-purpose flour, salt, and sugar to the berries. Stir gently to combine, trying not to mash the berries. Set the bowl to the side to allow the ingredients to combine.

In a medium bowl, add old fashioned rolled oats, flour, Speculaaskruiden, brown sugar and salt. Mix to incorporate.

Cut the stick of butter into small cubes and place them sporadically on top of the mixture. With your hands or a pastry cutter, cut the butter into the dry ingredients until the mixture is crumbly and the butter is well combined.

Lightly butter a 9x13" casserole pan or 12" cast iron skillet.

Spread the fruit mixture on the bottom of the dish. Sprinkle the crisp topping evenly over the top of the fruit mixture.

Bake for 45 minutes until the fruit mixture is bubbly and the crisp topping is golden brown.

When it is done, let it cool slightly for about 10-15 minutes. It will thicken as it cools.

Lenny loves serving his crisp with vanilla bean ice cream or fresh whipping cream. **Serves 6**

Streusel Topped Banana Bread

For Bread

3-4 very ripe or frozen (and thawed) bananas

½ c. brown sugar

1 c. white sugar

2 eggs

2/3 c. melted butter

1 tsp. vanilla (optional)

3 c. all-purpose flour

2 tsp. baking soda

2 tsp. baking powder

1 tsp. salt

For Streusel

2/3 c. brown sugar

4 Tbsp. flour

¼ tsp. cinnamon

2 Tbsp. softened butter

Banana Bread Instructions

Preheat oven to 350° F. Grease or line two loaf pans, or two 12-count muffin tins. As you can see in the photos, Lenny makes both muffins and loaves with this recipe.

Peel and mash the bananas with a fork. Add the two different sugars, eggs, butter, vanilla, baking soda, baking powder and salt. Lastly add the flour and stir till just incorporated. Pour the finished batter into the prepared pans or tins.

In a clean bowl, prepare the streusel. Add the butter, flour, cinnamon, and brown sugar. Stir till combined. It will be chunky and granulated. Sprinkle this on to of all the muffins or loaves.

Bake for 60 minutes or until a toothpick comes out clean. If the tops are browning too quickly, cover in tin foil. **Yields 2 Loaves or 24 Muffins**

RECIPE:_____

INGREDIENTS:_____

_____
_____
_____
_____
_____
_____
_____

INSTRUCTIONS:_____

_____
_____
_____
_____
_____
_____
_____
_____
_____
_____
_____
_____

TO AVOID SMUDGING, USE PERMENANT MARKER AND ALLOW ADEQUATE TIME TO
DRY INK.

RECIPE: _____

INGREDIENTS: _____

INSTRUCTIONS: _____

TO AVOID SMUDGING, USE PERMENANT MARKER AND ALLOW ADEQUATE TIME TO
DRY INK.

RECIPE:_____

INGREDIENTS:_____

INSTRUCTIONS:_____

TO AVOID SMUDGING, USE PERMENANT MARKER AND ALLOW ADEQUATE TIME TO DRY INK.

RECIPE: _____

INGREDIENTS: _____

_____
_____
_____
_____
_____
_____
_____
_____

INSTRUCTIONS: _____

_____
_____
_____
_____
_____
_____
_____
_____
_____
_____
_____
_____
_____
_____

TO AVOID SMUDGING, USE PERMENANT MARKER AND ALLOW ADEQUATE TIME TO
DRY INK.

RECIPE:_____

INGREDIENTS:_____
_____
_____
_____
_____
_____
_____

INSTRUCTIONS:_____
_____
_____
_____
_____
_____
_____
_____
_____
_____
_____
_____
_____
_____

TO AVOID SMUDGING, USE PERMENANT MARKER AND ALLOW ADEQUATE TIME TO
DRY INK.

RECIPE:_____

INGREDIENTS:_____

_____
_____
_____
_____
_____
_____
_____

INSTRUCTIONS:_____

_____
_____
_____
_____
_____
_____
_____
_____
_____
_____
_____
_____
_____
_____

TO AVOID SMUDGING, USE PERMENANT MARKER AND ALLOW ADEQUATE TIME TO DRY INK.

RECIPE:_____

INGREDIENTS:_____

_____
_____
_____
_____
_____
_____
_____

INSTRUCTIONS:_____

_____
_____
_____
_____
_____
_____
_____
_____
_____
_____
_____
_____
_____

TO AVOID SMUDGING, USE PERMENANT MARKER AND ALLOW ADEQUATE TIME TO DRY INK.

RECIPE: _____

INGREDIENTS: _____

_____
_____
_____
_____
_____
_____
_____

INSTRUCTIONS: _____

_____
_____
_____
_____
_____
_____
_____
_____
_____
_____
_____
_____
_____
_____

TO AVOID SMUDGING, USE PERMENANT MARKER AND ALLOW ADEQUATE TIME TO DRY INK.

RECIPE:_____

INGREDIENTS:_____

_____
_____
_____
_____
_____
_____

INSTRUCTIONS:_____

_____
_____
_____
_____
_____
_____
_____
_____
_____
_____
_____
_____
_____

TO AVOID SMUDGING, USE PERMENANT MARKER AND ALLOW ADEQUATE TIME TO DRY INK.

RECIPE: _____

INGREDIENTS: _____

_____
_____
_____
_____
_____
_____
_____

INSTRUCTIONS: _____

_____
_____
_____
_____
_____
_____
_____
_____
_____
_____
_____
_____
_____

TO AVOID SMUDGING, USE PERMENANT MARKER AND ALLOW ADEQUATE TIME TO
DRY INK.

Blend, Mash and Mix

Guacamole & Salsa

Guacamole

3 avocados mashed

1 Tbsp. lime juice

½ c. diced onion

½ c. cilantro

2 Roma tomatoes diced

1 tsp. garlic granules

¼ tsp. paprika

Pinch of Cayenne pepper

Pinch of ground cumin

Mash it all together!

Salsa

1 c. white onion

1 Serrano pepper

1 Tbsp. lime juice

1 Tsp. salt

6 diced Roma tomatoes

½ cup of cilantro

1 tsp. ground cumin

Mix and serve as is, or pulse in a blender.

Penny's Breakfast Smoothie

16oz milk of choice

4 Tbsp. almonds

2 servings chocolate protein powder

4 pitted dates

1 Tbsp. cocoa powder

2 bananas

Add all ingredients to a blender and mix till smooth and creamy.

Serves 2

Pina Colada Smoothie

1 banana

½ c. pineapple

½ c. mango

¼ c. riced cauliflower

1 cup coconut milk

1 handful ice

Squirt of lemon

Dash of cinnamon

Add all ingredients to a blender and mix till smooth. Lenny prefers to use mostly frozen ingredients in this recipe, but it is not required. Cauliflower adds an element of creaminess to the smoothie and you cannot even taste it! **Serves 2**

RECIPE:_____

INGREDIENTS:_____

_____
_____
_____
_____
_____
_____
_____

INSTRUCTIONS:_____

_____
_____
_____
_____
_____
_____
_____
_____
_____
_____
_____
_____
_____

TO AVOID SMUDGING, USE PERMENANT MARKER AND ALLOW ADEQUATE TIME TO
DRY INK.

RECIPE: _____

INGREDIENTS: _____

_____
_____
_____
_____
_____
_____
_____

INSTRUCTIONS: _____

_____
_____
_____
_____
_____
_____
_____
_____
_____
_____
_____
_____

TO AVOID SMUDGING, USE PERMENANT MARKER AND ALLOW ADEQUATE TIME TO DRY INK.

RECIPE:_____

INGREDIENTS:_____

INSTRUCTIONS:_____

TO AVOID SMUDGING, USE PERMENANT MARKER AND ALLOW ADEQUATE TIME TO DRY INK.

RECIPE: _____

INGREDIENTS: _____

INSTRUCTIONS: _____

TO AVOID SMUDGING, USE PERMENANT MARKER AND ALLOW ADEQUATE TIME TO DRY INK.

RECIPE:_____

INGREDIENTS:_____

_____
_____
_____
_____
_____
_____
_____

INSTRUCTIONS:_____

_____
_____
_____
_____
_____
_____
_____
_____
_____
_____
_____
_____

TO AVOID SMUDGING, USE PERMENANT MARKER AND ALLOW ADEQUATE TIME TO DRY INK.

RECICE: _____

INGREDIENTS: _____

_____
_____
_____
_____
_____
_____
_____

INSTRUCTIONS: _____

_____
_____
_____
_____
_____
_____
_____
_____
_____
_____
_____
_____

TO AVOID SMUDGING, USE PERMENANT MARKER AND ALLOW ADEQUATE TIME TO DRY INK.

RECIPE:_____

INGREDIENTS:_____

_____
_____
_____
_____
_____
_____

INSTRUCTIONS:_____

_____
_____
_____
_____
_____
_____
_____
_____
_____
_____
_____
_____

TO AVOID SMUDGING, USE PERMENANT MARKER AND ALLOW ADEQUATE TIME TO
DRY INK.

RECIPE: _____

INGREDIENTS: _____

_____
_____
_____
_____
_____
_____

INSTRUCTIONS: _____

_____
_____
_____
_____
_____
_____
_____
_____
_____
_____
_____
_____
_____

TO AVOID SMUDGING, USE PERMENANT MARKER AND ALLOW ADEQUATE TIME TO DRY INK.

RECIPE: _____

INGREDIENTS: _____

_____
_____
_____
_____
_____
_____
_____

INSTRUCTIONS: _____

_____
_____
_____
_____
_____
_____
_____
_____
_____
_____
_____
_____
_____

TO AVOID SMUDGING, USE PERMENANT MARKER AND ALLOW ADEQUATE TIME TO DRY INK.

Social & Inquires

Stay in Touch with Leonard!

Instagram: @whosagoodlizard

Please keep in touch with us on Instagram! Lenny is always releasing new recipes and dressing for obscure holidays. It is a fun way to keep up on national days, or just bring some positivity to your day!

Email: whosagoodlizard@gmail.com

Feel free to drop us an email! If you have any questions, comments or concerns about any of our recipes or would like to know how to make them fit your dietary needs, please reach out, and Lenny's culinary mentor/owner, will help you navigate through!

Many of the recipes can be made gluten free, vegan, dairy free etc. Do not hesitate to ask us how.

Have a request that is not in the book? Please email us! We love new ideas and challenges.